LIFE WITHIN US

Comprising

CHRIST WITHIN ME
Caryll Houselander

1957

JOURNEY INTO PRAYER
Delia Smith

1986

SURRENDER TO GOD
Herbert Fincham

1946

CATHOLIC TRUTH SOCIETY
PUBLISHERS TO THE HOLY SEE

Upon the world that seems
so cruel, mercy falls like
summer rain; upon the world
that seems so blind, light comes
down in living beams.

Caryll Houselander (1901-1954) was a writer and Catholic convert.
Delia Smith is a well-known television cook. Herbert Fincham
(ob. 1972) was a priest of Arundel and Brighton diocese.

CTS ONEFIFTIES

Originally published as: *Christ within Me*, 1957, adapted from a chapter in
The Passion of the Infant Christ (London, Sheed & Ward, 1949); *Journey into
Prayer*, 1986, previously published as a serial in *The Catholic Herald*; *Second
Conversion*, 1963, previously published as *Surrender to God*, 1946.
Published by The Incorporated Catholic Truth Society,
40-46 Harleyford Road, London SE11 5AY
www.ctsbooks.org
ISBN 978 1 78469 539 2

CHRIST WITHIN ME

Caryll Houselander

CHRIST WITHIN ME

Caryll Houselander

Christ's Abiding Presence in the Host

It would seem impossible, did we not know it to be true, that God could abide with us always, in littleness and humanity even more extreme than infancy. Or that His love should choose to give us the unity of His Birth and Death and Resurrection, always taking place at the heart of the world, from sunrise to sunset, and all life, and all love, always radiating from it.

Yet this is so. Every day, every hour, Christ is born on the altar in the hands of the priest; Christ is lifted up and sacrificed; Christ is buried in the tomb of the human heart; Christ rises from the tomb to be the life of the world through His Communion with men.

This is the Host-Life. Everything relates to the Host.

If we live the Host-Life in Christ we shall bring to life the contemplation of the Passion of the Infant Christ and live it in our own lives.

The Host is the Bread of Life. It is the good seed that the Sower sowed in His field; it is the harvest ready for the reaping.

It is the seed that is sown by the Spirit in every public way and every secret place on earth. It is the seed which, whenever it is buried, springs up from the grave to flower with everlasting life.

It is the mystery of the snowflake. It is the whiteness, the roundness, the littleness, which at once conceals and reveals the plan of Eternal Love.

It is the littleness, the dependence, the trust in human creatures of the Divine Infancy. It is the silence of the Child in the womb: the constriction of the swaddling-bands.

It is the Bread which is broken and yet is our wholeness. The wholeness of all that is. It is the breaking of the Bread which is the Communion of all men in Christ, in which the multiple lives of the world are one Christ-Life, the fragmentary sorrows of the world are one Christ-Passion, the broken loves of the world are one Christ-Love.

The Host seems to be divided among us; but, in reality, we, who were divided, are made one in the Host.

It is the obedience of childhood. The simplicity which is the singleness of childhood's love. It is the newness in which Heaven and earth are made new.

It is the birth of Christ in the nations; the restoring of the Christ-Child to the world; of childhood to the children.

With the dawning of this turbulent twentieth century came the children's Pope, St Pius X, to give Holy Communion to the little ones. In the hearts of the little children, Christ went out to meet Herod all over the world.

The Mass is the Birth and Death and Resurrection of Christ: in it is the complete surrender of those who love God.

The miracle of Cana takes place. The water of humanity is mixed into the wine and is lost in it. The wine is changed into the Blood of Christ.

In the offering of the bread and wine, we give material things as Our Lady gave her humanity to be changed into Christ. At the words of Consecration the bread and wine are not there any more; they simply *are not* any more but, instead, Christ is there.

In that which looks and tastes and feels like unleavened bread, Christ comes closer to us even than the infant could come, even than the child in the womb. He is our food, our life.

We give ourselves up to Him. He gives Himself up to us.

He is lifted up in the priest's hands, sacrificed. God accepts the sacrifice, and gives Christ back to us. He is lowered on to the altar; He who was taken down from the Cross is given to us in Communion; buried, laid to rest in our hearts.

It is His Will to rise from the dead in our lives and to come back to the world in His risen Host-Life.

In His risen life on earth Christ often made Himself recognized only by the characteristic of His unmistakable Love; by showing His wounds, by His infinite courtesy, by the breaking of bread. He would not allow the sensible beauty and dearness of His human personality, His familiar appearance, to hide the essential *Self* that He had come back to give.

Wholly consistent with this is Christ's return to us in the Host. We know that in it He is wholly present, Body, Blood, Soul, Divinity. But all this is hidden, even His human appearance is hidden. He insists, because this is the way of absolute love, in coming to us stripped of everything but Himself.

The Self-Stripping of Christ and Our Own Powerlessness

For this Self-giving Christ, in the Host, is poor, poorer than He was when, stripped of everything, He was naked on the Cross. He has given up even the appearance of His Body, the sound of His Voice, His power of mobility. He has divested Himself of colour and weight and taste. He has made Himself as close to nothing as He could be, while still being accessible to us.

In the Host He is the endless *Consummatum est* of the Passion of the Infant Christ.

In the Host He is our life on earth to-day.

There is no necessity for me to describe the average life. Too many know it. Countless millions have to make the way of the Cross and the way to Heaven through the same few streets, among the same tiny circle of people; through the same returning monotony; while many, many others have even less variety in their lives, less outward interest and less chance of active mercy or apostleship—those who are incurably ill, or in prison, or very old, confined not only to one town or village, but to one room, to one bed in a ward, to one narrow cell.

Everyone wants to take part in the healing and comforting

of the world, but most people are dogged by the sense of their own futility.

Even the power of genius and exceptional opportunity dwindles, measured against the suffering of our times. It is then hardly to be wondered at if the average person whose life is limited by narrow circumstances and personal limitations feels discouragement that is almost despair.

The Power of Christ's Love in Us

Living the Christ-Life means that we are given the power of Christ's Love. We are not only trustees of God's love for man, entrusted to give it out second-hand, but, miraculously, *our* love IS His love!

"I have bestowed My love upon you, just as My Father has bestowed His love upon Me. Live on then in My love…"

The Host-Life is an intense concentration of this power of love.

The Host-Life is not something new or different from the Christ-Life that we know already. It is the very core of it, and it was given to us at the Last Supper when Christ gave Himself to us in the Blessed Sacrament.

The Host-Life is the life which Christ Himself is living in the world now. It is His choice of how to live His life among us to-day. At first sight it is baffling that it should be so.

Have *you* never stood before the Tabernacle and asked yourself: "Why is He silent, while the world rocks with blasphemies and lies? Why is He passive while His followers are persecuted and innocent people are crushed?"

It is almost frightening to seek an answer to the question: "Why does God remain in our midst silent and passive, knowing and seeing everything, but saying and doing nothing, while cruelty, injustice, ignorance and misery go on and on and on?"

It is a frightening question until we remember what it is which alone *can* restore humanity to happiness; that it is one thing only that can do it, namely supernatural life, beginning secretly in each individual heart; just as Incarnate Love began secretly in each individual heart; just as Incarnate Love began secretly on earth in the heart of Mary. It is one thing only, the birth of the Infant Christ in us, Incarnate Love.

No voice of warning could effect this. That could make men tremble; it could not make them love. No armed force could do it, not even supernatural force. That could make men slaves: love is always free.

Love must begin from within. It must be sown in the inmost darkness of the human heart, and take root and flower from the dust that man is.

This can only happen if the Holy Spirit descends from Heaven and penetrates human nature, as the rays of the sun and summer rain come down into the earth, warming and irrigating the seed that is sown there and quickening it.

Christ sowed the seed of His life in us when He sowed the world with drops of His Blood from the Cross. Now it is Christ in the Host who draws down the Holy Spirit. For the Holy Spirit is the Eternal Love between the Father and the Son. Love which cannot resist the plea of the silence, the patience, the obedience of the Sacred Host.

Christ Lives in Us

In the Host Christ gives Himself to live the ordinary life as it is to-day, to live it fully in all its essentials, and to take into Himself, into His own living of the Host-Life, the most ordinary, the most numerous, seemingly the most mediocre lives, bestowing upon them His own power to bring down the Spirit of Love.

In those who have received Him in Holy Communion, Christ goes among whom He will, to whatever places He chooses to be in: with little children He goes into the schoolroom; with office workers, to the office; with shop assistants, to the shop. Everyone with whom the communicant has even a passing contact during the day is someone whom Christ wished to meet. Not only priests, but doctors and nurses and the servants and paper sellers in hospitals take Him to the sick and the dying; to patients who have forgotten God. Not only the military chaplain, but common soldiers take Him into the barracks and into battle. In their comrades Christ marches side by side with boys who have never been told about His Love. He walks in their footsteps.

An unknown martyr priest of our own times, whose anointed hands had been cut off by his persecutors so that he might never again consecrate bread and wine, sent this message secretly from his exile, asking his friends to take it from one to another round the world:

"I can never again carry the Sacred Host or lift It up in my hands, but no one can prevent me from carrying Our Lord in my heart wherever I am. You, who are not prisoners, who are not held in one place, go often to Holy Communion, carry Christ everywhere in your hearts, make your souls monstrances, and go into those places where Our Lord has never been adored in the Host, where the monstrance has never been lifted up."

Christ in Others Awaits our Love

How often we think that but for this or that person in our lives we should be saints! That troublesome person in the office; that exasperating fellow-lodger; that spiteful old relative who is on our back like the old man of the sea! They are our stumbling blocks. Why is it allowed? Why is it that we cannot get away from them?

It is because Christ wishes to be with them and has chosen us to take Him to them. He loves them, He sees the depths of their loneliness: He has plumbed it with His love. *Moreover, He approaches us in them.* They bring Him to us in just that aspect that He wishes to be known to us. His presence in them may save us from some particular sin. They may be, to us, Christ forgiving, Christ in His patience, Christ teaching. They may be Christ in His weariness, or Christ in His fear in Gethsemani, Christ facing His death. They may come dependent and helpless as Christ in His childhood or infancy. They may come as Christ in that particular need of His to which our response means our salvation. Possibly the neglected Christ in the Tabernacle to whom we have made such fervent promises of reparation, such acts of self-dedication, still awaits our rudimentary courtesy, unrecognized, unloved and lonely under our own roof.

It takes our breath away to think of Christ's self-giving in the Host. We hardly realize it, because it is so amazing that to speak realistically of it demands a daring that sounds like blasphemy to our unaccustomed ears.

Christ's Silence and Obedience in the Host

In the Host Christ is silent—in fact voiceless, dependent, even helpless. He is carried in the hands of men wherever they choose. His obedience is beyond death.

Think how aptly countless lives approximate to the Host. In His silence how many there are who must endure in silence; who, sometimes in tragic circumstances, have no opportunity to plead their cause. How many, too, are silent through fear. Fear that complaint may cost them a detested but necessary job. Fear of ridicule, like new children at boarding-school, or boys and girls in the throes of first love. How many there are who are dumb-hearted, inarticulate, unable to express themselves, or who, though they long to unburden their minds to a fellow-creature, never find a willing or sympathetic listener. And there is the religious silence, the "Great Silence" of Religious Houses, in which men and women bring their whole will to entering into the silence of the Host.

In His dependence and helplessness surely every one, at the beginning and end of life, is included, children, and old people in their last illness; and on any given day — since the supernatural life must be lived out fully *every* day — all those filling the crowded hospitals of the world.

In His obedience; there are vast numbers of people who are subject to others — workers, soldiers, sailors and airmen, hospital nurses, inmates of institutions, prisoners, children. With, few exceptions, everyone.

In the light of the Host-Life, shining upon the modern world, it becomes clearly visible that the power of love, of comforting, of healing and alleviating suffering is given to the most unlikely people; to those who seem to be the most restricted: that the most effective action belongs to those who seem helpless and unable to do anything at all, and that there is a tremendous force of contemplation, unrecognized, but redeeming, in the midst of the secular world.

But it would be presumptuous to suppose that the mere fact of narrow, limiting circumstances is all that is required. No one is excluded from this contemplation in action. The genius as well as the simpleton can enter into the Host-Life, because it does not depend first of all upon outward things, but upon interior things.

Our Surrender, the Condition of Christ's Life in Us

The condition on our side is surrender as complete as that which we learn from the service of the Divine Infant; unreserved surrender of self to the life of Christ in the Host.

Surrender to Christ as complete as His surrender to us in the Host-Life.

It is seldom, when *much* is asked for, that human nature fails to respond. It is when too little (as we think) is asked of us, when we have little to offer, that we fail; when the offering seems too slight or too fragmentary; something absurd in the face of the Eternal Love that consecrates it, and the immensity of the human suffering that needs it.

Our Offerings Never too Small

In every normal lifetime certain days stand out when some crisis, such as acute pain or danger, integrates, points and concentrates the offering of self; when, momentarily, human nature is vested in a little majesty, and so the idea of immolation seems less absurd. But in the ordinary way it seems futile.

In spite of the heaviness with which they afflict us personally, we have, after all, such trifles to offer; boredom, hurt vanity, uncongenial environment, self-consciousness, little aches and pains, trifling disappointments, brief embarrassments, half-imaginary fear and anxieties. We can hardly believe that God accepts these!

Christ has forestalled all that. The offering to be changed into His Flesh is the most fragile wafer of unleavened bread, light as the petal of a rose; flexible, colourless, only just substance at all. It is made out of tiny separate grains. It is *this* that Christ chooses for His supreme miracle of love. Moreover, He chooses that it shall be offered every

15

day anew. That every day this offering shall be changed into His Body.

A Daily Sacrifice

We are asked to offer only what we have, what we are to-day. That it is so little means nothing: it is our wafer of unleavened bread.

If we are troubled by the fact that we are not at one with ourselves, that we are full of conflict and distraction, that we have not even achieved singleness of heart sufficient for one perfect prayer, that we are broken up by distractions, by scattered thoughts, emotions, desires, we must realize that our offering, too, begins by being many separate grains.

We must take one grain, the nearest at hand; a momentary joy, a particular anxiety, a slight discomfort, an aching limb, an embarrassment, and offer that. But in order to offer that, our whole self must be gathered in, integrated in the offering. The offering cannot possibly be made otherwise.

We must bring our minds to it, our will, our heart. We must close our thoughts round it, at least for a second, in a shining circle. Thus the offering itself integrates us: in it the scattered grains of our life become one bread.

Imitating Christ in the Host literally, we must make our offering daily, not grieving at the failure of yesterday, but through the offering of to-day, being made new to-day, and this every day.

The Rest of Christ in the Host

The Host is Rest. Still, infinite Peace. In this rest is the mysterious activity of Love. It is the rest of the love between the Persons of the Blessed Trinity.

It is the rest of Christ on earth.

It is Christ's rest in Advent: the silence, the dependence, the secrecy of the unborn. In the Host-Life men contribute to this rest by giving themselves to be Himself, as Our Lady gave herself. It is the rest of surrender.

It is Christ's rest by the well, when He asked the woman of Samaria for a drink of water. The rest of the Human Christ, who allows Himself to be tired for our sake and asks for refreshment. It is the rest that asks for reparation, for the cup of cold water, for which Christ will give back the living water of immortality. It is the rest of the Humility which allowed the woman, a sinful woman at that, to achieve through His weariness what He Himself did not achieve through His power: the conversion of a whole village.

It is the rest of Christ sleeping in the boat, while the storm terrified His Apostles. It is the Faith which enables the children of God to sleep on His Heart while the storm of evil and suffering rocks the world around them.

It is the rest of Christ in the tomb, the profound rest of Communion, when Christ is laid in the human heart and asks of those who receive Him there Silence, Darkness, Death. Silence, which is the stillness of the heart at Holy Communion, not broken by fear or thought or wilfulness: the wordless silence of trust. The silence of the trust of the

Father into whose hands we commit not only our little life, comparable to a sparrow's life and the life of grass, but the Real Life, Christ in us, our Being. The silence of the lips closed upon the *Consummatum est*!

The Darkness is the darkness of Faith which is content to see nothing, to feel nothing; the darkness and obliteration of the senses, the Faith which asks for no reassurance, no sign of the Divine Presence, no stir of life in the sown field. The Faith which accepts the appearance in which the Divine life is concealed in the Host as its own soul's portion, and is content without colour or odour or sound or taste.

The Death is the death of self. In this death the life of self which is the life of corruption, the restlessness of the worms in a corpse, ceases in silence and darkness; in this death is peace; like the peace which embalmed the dead Christ in the tomb. All the sweetness that is foregone is the precious ointment spilt out of the broken alabaster box for Christ's burial: what is left in the box is emptiness; the spikenard is there to comfort the wounded Body of Love.

The spikenard, that lovely waste, is, as we have seen, one with the frankincense and myrrh poured out for the Divine Infant. The Rest of Christ in the tomb of our hearts is the sleeping of the seed in winter. The Midnight of Bethlehem is the Morning of Resurrection.

Thanksgiving, Our Supreme Prayer

Holy Communion — the Holy Eucharist — is thanksgiving. Ultimately our Trust, our Faith, our Peace, is all summed up in Thanksgiving, Thanksgiving to our Heavenly Father for His Son, His Gift to us.

Present at our Thanksgiving are the angels. We enter into Christ's rest again in the presence of the angels. We are in the Eternal moments in the Wilderness and in Gethsemani, when in His unimaginable humility Christ leaned upon the comforting of His holy angels. May our own guardian angels, who are with us in temptation and with us in the Gethsemani of the world's agony to-day, be with us in our thanksgiving, fending the flame of Christ's life in us with their spread wings, folding them upon our peace, to comfort Him in our souls. May they roll back the stone at the door of the tomb of our hearts that, every day, Christ in whom we die may rise from the dead in us and go back, in our lives, to the world.

The Crucifixion was public; the shame, the humiliation, the mockery, were seen by the crowd. Just as it is now. The Resurrection and the Risen life were secret; then, as now, to be discovered gradually and individually in each life, according to the individual necessity of love. The Glory of the Host is hidden, seen only by God. The Glory of the Host-Life is hidden too, a secret apostolate, a secret Kingdom of Heaven on earth.

The Hidden Transformation of the World

There is no outward sign of the miracle that is taking place. Office workers are bending over their desks, mothers working in their kitchens, patients lying quietly in hospital wards, nurses carrying out the exacting routine of their work of mercy, craftsmen are at their benches, factory workers riveted to their machines, prisoners are in their cells, children in their schools. In the country, farmers rise with the sun and go out to work on the land until sunset; the farm wives are feeding, milking, churning, cooking for their men and their children. Everywhere an unceasing rhythm of toil, monotonous in its repetition, goes on.

To those inside the pattern of love that it is weaving it seems monotonous in its repetition, it seems to achieve very little.

In the almshouses and the workhouses old people, who are out of the world's work at last, sit quietly with folded hands. It seems to them that their lives add up to very little too.

Nowhere is there any visible sign of glory. But, because in every town and village and hamlet of the world there are those who have surrendered their lives to the Host-Life, who have made their offering daily from the small grains of the common life, a miracle of love is happening all the time everywhere. The Holy Spirit is descending upon the world. There is Incarnation everywhere — everywhere the Infant Christ is born; every day the Infant Christ makes the world new.

Upon the world that seems so cruel, mercy falls like summer rain; upon the world that seems so blind, light comes down in living beams. The heart of man that seems so hard, is sifted, irrigated, warmed; the water of life floods it. The fire and light of the Spirit burn in it. The seed of Christ-Life, which seemed to have dried up, lives and quickens, and from the secret depths of man's being the Divine Life flowers.

JOURNEY INTO PRAYER

Delia Smith

JOURNEY INTO PRAYER

Delia Smith

ONE

If I were to be given just one word with which to communicate the seemingly complicated subject of prayer, the word I would choose is *simplicity*. Simplicity is the key that opens the door of obscurity to let in the clear breeze of God's wisdom and refresh our jaded minds.

It is on just such a refreshing note that the author of the Book of Wisdom opens: 'Seek the Lord in simplicity of heart, since he is to be found by those who do not put him to the test.' There, in a nutshell, is the whole subject of prayer.

If we are seeking God with that pure simplicity of heart, then we are utterly sure of finding him. Wasn't that his great promise to us: 'Those who seek always find' (Luke 11)? As we seek him, so shall we find him in the same measure, and finding him we shall come to know him—not in a vague, notional way but in a deepening, intimate way.

Prayer, then, is a journey into faith, a faith which grows and develops along the way like (to use the familiar metaphor) the tiny seed hidden in the earth and growing in darkness: though we do not see it, we await its blossoming.

As the measure of our knowing God increases, so does our faith; and as we know him so we learn to trust him. The pinnacle of faith is total trust, and anyone who has scaled this pinnacle has found heaven on earth, because the fruit of total trust is 'the peace that passes all understanding'.

In the office of readings for Lent the Church reminds us of this spiritual journey to which we are all individually called by following the great Exodus story. For that is a journey of faith we can follow today: we are called out of slavery into the wilderness of faith, we learn to confront our enemies and trust in the God who goes before us to the promised land of peace.

In that stubborn band of Hebrews we can see ourselves, often incredulous, too easily content to live with oppression rather than risk the journey. Their journey, like ours, was filled with mistakes and failures and painfully highlighted the limits of human nature.

Yet at the same time, what hope this story holds out! In it we can see how God deals with our incapacity. When they failed to believe, and failed to trust, he tried again. His relentless love reaches out to draw us into a relationship. Listen how clearly scripture describes his role in that journey: 'In the waste lands [unbelief] he adopts us; in the lowly deserts of the wilderness [our darkness] he protects us, rears us, guards us as the apple of his eye. Like an eagle watching its nest, hovering over its young, he spreads out his wings to hold us and support us' (Deut.32).

The spiritual journey is one in which we learn by experience how to grasp this love with certainty. But we can only arrive at that point if we have the will to make the journey at all. However inadequate we feel, somewhere deep within us we must *want* to make it.

Of course, like the Hebrews, we lack faith—but note: they only learn *on the way*. It is only the experience of the reality of God's promise that fortifies them in faith in spite of repeated failures. When we have seen the Red Sea parted— or something similar—in our own lives, only then can we grasp God's power and learn to trust.

God sent Moses as mediator between him and his people, but in our age he has come himself. By sharing our pain and frustrations and helplessness, and by knowing what human sorrow is, Jesus teaches us as we are and where we are. His words to one who was about to embark on this journey are words for each of us: 'If you only knew what God is offering, and who it is who asks you…!'

Like the Hebrews, and the woman at the well, we cannot know until we start and learn to know who Jesus is and what he is offering. The woman at the well takes the first step by making a decision: 'Give me some water.'

That's our decision too. Do we want to know God? Do we want to receive what he is offering? Will we follow him like the sheep in John 10, who learn to 'know' his voice? Will we allow him to lead us across the desert of our lives?

Jesus's own explanation to his disciples says a great deal to me about the nature of prayer: 'If anyone loves me he will keep my word, and my Father will love him, and we shall come to him and make our home in him.'

If anyone loves me: this is the decision for God. Love is not a way of feeling but a commitment, a two-way commitment, a covenant relationship as it was on Mount Sinai.

And we shall come to him: Prayer is not something achieved by our own effort but something received once we have made the commitment.

And make our home in him: By desiring God, by listening to his word and allowing it to penetrate, I am opening myself to that encounter where my spirit is touched by the spirit of the living God himself—so that I gradually become infused with his own life. It is a process enshrined in that most beautiful of prayers, 'Come Holy Spirit and enkindle in me the fire of your love.' Then each individual life that surrenders to this journey, this process of becoming infused with the life of God, becomes part of his new creation which furthers the renewal of the face of the earth and the coming of his kingdom.

TWO

But this is the *end* of the story. Now let's go back to the beginning. Prayer begins with a decision. True prayer isn't possible unless there comes a moment in our lives when we consciously *choose* to want to know God. Like the woman at the well, we may not know exactly what we want, but somewhere deep within us we turn towards him for the answer.

To understand how this happens I think we first need to reflect on what—in a personal sense—can bring about this decision. Every single human life is a unique and special gift of God's fashioning: he is intimately involved in the fabric of our being, forming and shaping our lives, continuing the work of our creation.

We can know this in truth yet be unable to grasp the mystery: like the psalmist we have to concede 'too wonderful for me is this knowledge'. The awesomeness of this gift, each individual human life, has to be reflected on—and prayer begins with reflection.

Consider the miracle of your own life. No-one who has ever lived has had a face, or a voice, quite like yours; the very imprint of your thumb is a mark of your individuality and complexity.

You are like a rare and precious gem that cannot be

matched. Once again the psalmist is intuitively catching the awesomeness of the gift of his own creation when he cries out: 'I thank you, God, that *I am wonderful!*'

The simple truth is that God created you because he wanted *you* exactly as you are, and, as you are, to have a relationship with you.

In this relationship we start out, in Paul's descriptive words, as empty vessels. But that empty vessel, which is me, has unlimited capacity because my life—again in Paul's words—has the capacity (if I enter into that relationship) to be filled with the utter 'fullness of God'.

This is what we need to grasp if we are going to look at the roots of what eventually becomes a decision for God. The empty space will be experienced as a sense of incompleteness, a deep yearning for something we cannot put into words.

It is an experience beyond the level of senses, of hunger or thirst or sexual feelings. It is really that I *want* something but I don't know what it is. It creates an inner tension, a feeling of dissatisfaction that I have described elsewhere as a 'deep-down ache'.

There are ways of anaesthetising that ache: by seeking satisfaction in other things, by creating god-substitutes, 'carved idols' to use the biblical image. There are bigger and lesser idols, work, frantic activity, ambition, material gain, sport, perfection in the house or garden…all good things, all God's gifts, but how subtly they can dominate our lives in our attempt to fill the aching void.

Sometimes as we get older, and perhaps achieve our goals,

we begin to get an inkling that things don't measure up and satisfy us in the way we thought they would. The ache begins to resurface and again we face our lack of fulfilment. Many people are very vulnerable at this stage. Perhaps they drive themselves harder, or drink more, or take drugs, or have affairs. In her inspiring book *To Believe in Jesus* Ruth Burrows explains it like this: 'What from the outside seems to us sin and wickedness, is not so in God's eyes. Is it any more, I wonder, than the frantic screaming of a child in the frightening darkness of the night?'

For the prodigal son it was necessary for him to plumb the very depths of his darkness before he could make that all-important decision to journey back into relationship with his father.

For many of us the decision won't be so dramatic. It will take a lifetime. But until we breathe our very last breath God will be patiently—relentlessly—'standing at the door and knocking', awaiting our decision to open up and allow him to fill us with the life he longs to give us.

We cannot attempt to begin the journey of faith and prayer until we *have* made this decision. St Teresa of Avila said it's not with many words that he hears us but in the silence of our longing. It has nothing to do with the outward show of religion, or being a person of high principles and good works. He can 'hear' our longing from the gutter, as he did when the woman washed his feet with her tears.

If we feel inadequate, Jesus himself has a reassuring little story about prayer. 'Two men went into the temple to pray…' it begins. The one who was doing all the right things didn't know either himself or God: he was practising religion not faith. The other man was in touch with his own dire needs, 'he hardly dared raise his eyes'. Yet *he* had discovered his own longing: in his wretched state he had come to the temple *to pray*. What hope this story holds out for us. For Jesus said that this was the man who went home at rights with God.

Prayer, then, begins with this all-important decision for God, a decision in which we are prepared to begin reflecting on the meaning of our existence, and get in touch with that inner longing, that 'hunger and thirst' that he alone can satisfy. For he has promised: 'He who comes to me will never be hungry, he who believes in me will never thirst' (John 6).

THREE

Having made the all-important decision to begin to seek a deeper personal relationship with God in prayer, the next stage of our spiritual journey is to ask how, in a practical way, can I seek him and know him?

The answer is deceptively simple. I say deceptively because to grasp it we need to be very simple ourselves.

The whole theme of the Bible is of God constantly reaching out to draw people into relationship. We must try to understand that in some inexplicable way our desire for God is inspired by his own desire for us, and that it is he who is the initiator of the relationship. We can see this relentless pursuit enacted in the history of Israel, and how we can interpret it on a personal level.

The theme of the fourth Eucharistic prayer illuminates this process: God forms us in his own likeness. Even when we disobey him, and lose his friendship he never abandons us but helps us to seek and find him. Again and again he offers us a covenant (relationship); through prophets he teaches us to hope for salvation. The climax of the prayer is God's desire for us (He 'so loved the world that in the fullness of time…').

God has actually provided us with the simplest way of knowing who he is—by coming to teach us himself. Through

Jesus we have access to all that God wants to teach us about himself. By sharing our poverty, our frail human nature, God has made himself totally accessible, teaching us on a human level how to have a relationship.

Isaiah caught this wonderful vision: '...they will be taught by God' (ch.54), the same passage that Jesus quotes, telling us how 'to hear the teaching of the Father, and to learn from it is to come to me'.

To know God, then, we must know and learn from Jesus—it's as simple as that. Like the disciples on the road to Emmaus we can learn to recognise him in the breaking of bread, the Mass, and in the Scriptures. Just as Jesus showed them that everything written in the Bible was about himself (Luke 24) and 'opened their minds to understand the Scriptures', so will he for us if we are truly seeking him. God is initiator and teacher: we are the recipients. As Paul wrote to the Corinthians, 'It's all God's work.'

So what must we do to receive this gift of intimate relationship through prayer? First, we must have the right attitude—which means not setting out to do something for God, but rather allowing him to do something for us.

But then, and most important, we must set aside time, prime time. It is impossible to have a relationship with anyone unless you're prepared to spend real time with them. So it is with God. Reflection is only possible when we have provided ourselves with space.

The enemy of prayer is activity. When Moses came to tell the Hebrews the good news of their redemption from slavery, Pharoah (their adversary) responds with the edict 'increase their work so that they have no time to listen'. The adversary's work has changed little today, and we can so easily become slaves to activity—which is why I emphasise the importance of a decision for God. It's only when I really want God that I will find time.

'When you pray,' Jesus says, 'go into your private room, and when you have shut the door, pray to your Father.' We can, of course, begin reflecting during the normal spaces of everyday life (train journeys, walking, driving, etc.) but sooner or later we have to set aside real time to be alone in the presence of God, in the simple words of the Psalmist, to 'be still and know God'. Jesus himself revealed time and again how necessary this was to him, by going off by himself to pray.

To start with, prayer is a matter of disciplining our lives, working out our priorities in order to make this precious time. At the beginning we can start with half-an-hour a day, but then our goal should be to work towards an hour given exclusively to God. It takes—according to American psychologists—eighteen months to form a new habit, so we must pray for patience and persevere until it has become a habit and a normal part of our daily lives.

One of the obstacles is very often fear: we fear we're not good enough, our minds are full of our problems and anxieties. But we must summon enough faith to believe that it is precisely here, in the midst of our human struggles, that God comes to us. 'Come to me all you who labour and are heavy-burdened and I will give you rest.' God, we should always remember, is not separated from the world; in the Gospels it is sinners that Jesus keeps company with.

Having found our space we need then to learn not just to read, but to listen to the word of God in scripture, taking a little at a time and allowing it to penetrate (in the Hebrew sense, that means learning to listen with the heart). What is so liberating about this is that you don't have to *do* anything, but allow the word to live, the active word of God do something to you, to touch you, to enlighten the eyes of your mind.

This is where the simplicity we talked of at the beginning comes in. The Pharisee's problem was that he needed to *be* somebody to offer God something; the publican, who went home at rights with God, had empty hands. To pray we need to be simple and receptive, to have the attitude of a little child. St Therese of Lisieux understood this: 'I expect nothing of myself,' she said, 'but everything of God.'

If we are willing to fight to find time for God, and if we're humble enough to listen and allow his word to touch our inmost hearts, then we are truly praying at the deepest level—letting prayer happen, letting God infuse our lives with his own. It is a touch that heals deaf ears and blind eyes, and awakens hearts to the newness of resurrected life that is eternal.

> When our hearts are wintry, grieving or in pain,
> your touch can call back to life again
> fields of our hearts that dead and bare have been,
> love is come again like wheat that springeth green.
>
> (Easter hymn)

FOUR

'Oh come to the water all you who are thirsty. Come
to me and listen to my words, hear me and you shall
have life' (Isaiah 55:3).

We started out on these short meditations on prayer by
underlining the need for simplicity, because it is simplicity
that provides us with a short cut on the spiritual journey. If
we reflect on the words of scripture above (the words that
are read out during the Easter Vigil) and compare them with
Jesus's own words in John 8, 'if you make my word your
home, you will learn the truth and the truth will make you
free,' we have all the instructions we need to set out on that
journey of faith which is prayer.

Hear! Listen! The words echo through the scriptures. If
we *want* to know God, to receive the life he longs to give
us, we must find the time in our lives to listen: we must
learn to listen not just with our ears but with our hearts.
God, we have to remember, alone is our spiritual director
and guide, and our role is one of receptivity. In the Old
Testament conversion (or a decision for God) is likened to
circumcision of the heart—as though a hairline crack were
being formed in my deepest centre which begins to open
me up to receptivity. Then, if I am prepared to find time

to listen to the word of God, my capacity to listen with the heart will grow at ever-deepening levels.

In the process of this gradual awakening to the living presence of God in his Word, I will discover the truth of the Book of Revelation: 'If anyone *hears my voice* and opens the door, I will come in and share his meal *side by side.*' The same idea—that the word of God renders our own striving unnecessary—occurs in the Old Testament too. 'No, the word is very near to you' it says in Deuteronomy. 'It is in your mouth and in your heart for your observance.' We don't have to wonder how we are going to climb to heaven, or cross oceans, to find it. St Augustine, in his own awakening, expressed the truth of it like this: 'For behold you were within me and I outside…you were with me but I was not with you.'

The disciples on the road to Emmaus did not recognise their side-by-side companion, but they *did* listen to him as he explained the scriptures. When they finally recognised him, then they understood how all the time 'their hearts had burned within them'. Simply by listening to the word, they had been awakened to their desire for God who dwells within. This is the indwelling of the Holy Spirit that Jesus referred to when he said to his disciples: 'You *know* him because he is with you, he is in you.'

Can we be simple enough to believe? We have the witness of others who believed in this simplicity: St Thérèse of Lisieux desired to go the whole way with God and become a saint, but she also accepted her own human limitations. If it was to happen, then only God could bring it about. Instead of trying to climb the steep slope to the spiritual summit purely by her own efforts, she asked God to provide her with a lift! In other words, if she was going to get there, God would have to carry her there himself!

To summarise the most significant landmarks on the journey of prayer:

First, do we want God? If we do then we will be prepared to seek to know him by providing time and space in our lives to listen to his word in scripture (and in particular the gospels).

As we seek him, so we shall find him (Luke 11), and as we find him so will our faith increase. The work involved in creating this time and space for listening and reflection will be like building a house on a solid rock-like foundation: if we succeed our growth in faith will be able to withstand the traumas of everyday life (the psalmist's 'storms of destruction'), and we will retain a deep peace and serenity whatever the disturbances on the surface.

Finally, as we grow in this intimate relationship with God which we call prayer, and gradually learn to respond to the spirit dwelling within us, so we shall receive the 'life' promised in Isaiah. Jesus reiterates this promise: 'If a man is thirsty [wanting God], let him come to me [relationship through prayer]. Let the man come and drink who believes in me [faith]. From his breast shall flow fountains of living water' (John 7).

In short, whoever makes the commitment to seek God in prayer will receive life, God's life that manifests itself in love.

Prayer is ultimately a journey into loving, where first of all we learn to love God (by commitment not by feelings), and as we learn to love him so in turn we learn to receive his love, and to love ourselves. Then we are truly free to love others, not in a forced, 'striving' way but with an instinctive love that is inspired by God's own relentless love for us.

Let's end with one of the most beautiful prayers in scripture, Paul's prayer for the Ephesians, which in its simplicity encapsulates all I have tried to say in these meditations:

> May he give you the power through his Spirit for your hidden self to grow strong, so that Christ may live in your hearts through faith, and then, planted in love and built on love, you will with all the saints have strength to grasp the breadth and length, the height and depth, until knowing the love of Christ, which is beyond all knowledge, you are filled with the utter fullness of God.
>
> (Ephesians 3, 16-19.)

SECOND CONVERSION

Herbert C. Fincham

SECOND CONVERSION

Herbert Finchman

If Much has been written and said on what is commonly called the 'leakage', and it has for the most part been rightly attributed to circumstances such as the lack of a good Catholic upbringing, lax example in the home, mixed marriages, and possible faults in the way the Faith is taught to children. Nevertheless there remain a fair number of defections among souls who have no such excuses. Some who have had the advantage of a good Catholic home and education, and who have shown more than average devotion to their religion, fall away, and it may be helpful to enquire into what appears likely to be at least one of the occasions of these failures.

A Spiritual Experience

Some may have experienced just such a crisis as a result of the war, but the spiritual experience about to be described is not confined to times of war and upheaval, for, I believe, all earnest souls, whose religion is more than a mere formality, must pass through it in some form or other. Our modern unrest may precipitate it and make it take a more obvious and even violent form. This in itself is not a bad thing though it adds to its dangers. It is a good thing in so far as it makes the crisis more marked and the act of the will, which is its proper culmination, more definite. The danger is that the soul may not be so well habituated in the practices of religion as it would be in later life, and thus can throw off religious exercises and even duties more easily.

We speak of our spiritual *life* and that is the first point that must be stressed and realized. *Grace is Life.* Our Lord never uses the word 'grace' but speaks incessantly of Life. He came to give us life. 'I come that they may have life and may have it more abundantly' (Jn 10:10). By Baptism we are born again into this new life (Jn 3:5). Now there is one very obvious thing about all life: that it must grow and develop. Moreover it must develop proportionately in its different parts and aspects, for example, in human life, in body, mind, and will. Without this proportion a person becomes in some way defective. He may have a child's mind and an adult body and thus be mentally deficient; or he may have the body of a child and a grown-up mind and be a precocious prodigy (which is almost worse than the former!); or he may as a full grown man still show the irresponsibility of a child and be a nuisance to everybody.

Definite Stages in Life

Again, we observe in natural life a few definite stages: infancy, childhood, puberty, youth, and manhood. These do not come suddenly so that we can point to the exact hour or day when a person passes from one to the other, but they have their own discernible characteristics and can be easily recognized when they have been reached. All these essential characteristics of normal life have their counterparts in the new supernatural life of the soul. For this reason Père Garrigou-Lagrange O.P. says: 'It is not surprising to find that the development of the interior life has often been compared to the three periods or stages of physical life: childhood, youth, and manhood. St Thomas himself has indicated this analogy: and it is an analogy which is worth pursuing, particular attention being paid to the transition from one period to another'. *(The Three Ways of the Spiritual Life.* Burns Oates & Washbourne Ltd. 1938. pp.25–26.)

By Baptism we receive the new supernatural life of the soul which we call Sanctifying Grace, and this is the first great conversion of the soul to God. It is, of course, the most important conversion of all but it is not the only one. By it we are turned to God and away from sin and the devil. We accept God as our Supreme Lord and Master by renouncing the devil with all his works and pomps. An infant makes this act of homage by proxy through the God-parents, and God gives the new supernatural life with His gifts of Faith, Hope, and Charity. Provided that the child is brought up properly in the Catholic Faith these infused gifts will preserve and develop the New Life of the soul while the habits of religious duties and practices are formed. There should be the normal growth from infancy to childhood when what is called the use of reason begins to dawn.

A Counterpart

This first stage of human development has its counterpart in the spiritual life of the soul, but it may not take place at the same point of time. None of the stages of physical and spiritual growth coincide chronologically but may be very distantly separated. There are many adults who appear not to have passed beyond their spiritual infancy or spiritual childhood. Very few reach the perfection of spiritual manhood. By 'spiritual infancy' and 'spiritual childhood' I am not, of course, referring to that perfection of holiness which our Lord enjoins for all souls when He says: 'Amen, I say to you, unless you be converted and become as little children, you shall not enter into the kingdom of heaven' (Matt. 18:3). This is an essential characteristic of all true spirituality, but in describing the growth of the spiritual life many writers use the expression 'spiritual childhood' to mark a stage in that development. It is in this sense that I am using it in this pamphlet.

The stage of spiritual childhood is manifested by the first dawning of some realization of the all-importance of religion and an implicit desire for spiritual progress. This development is essential before any further progress can be made and the next clearly discernible stage or crisis can be reached, which is the counterpart of the physical age of puberty and is often called, by spiritual writers, the Second Conversion. 'The important thing to be noticed is that, just as there is the crisis of puberty, more or less manifest and more or less successfully surpassed, between childhood and adolescence, so in the spiritual life there is an analogous crisis for the transition from the purgative life of beginners to the illuminative life of proficients. This crisis has been described by several great spiritual writers, in particular by Tauler and especially by St John of the Cross, under the name of the *passive purgation of the senses*, and by Père Lallemant S.J. and several others under the name of the *second conversion.*' (Père Garrigou-Lagrange O.P., op. cit, p.28.)

This *second conversion* is the subject of this pamphlet, for, in my opinion, it may well be the occasion of the falling away of souls who have passed from spiritual infancy to spiritual childhood and have shown more than average devotion to their religion. It may be a real help to souls in the throes of this crisis to have a short account of what they are experiencing and the reasons for it. Once it is fully realized that it is neither abnormal nor evil, there should be very much less danger of failure to pass through it successfully.

A Result of Original Sin

During our spiritual infancy and childhood the act of homage, made at Baptism, has never been fully comprehended in all its implications or renewed with the full and complete surrender which God has a right to demand from His creatures. This is precisely the reason for the Second Conversion, which is the full and explicit conversion or turning of our will by unconditional surrender to His perfect will. As a result of original sin our will tends to bear away from God and has to be drawn back, as it were, against its tension. This can be done only by the grace of God, but grace needs the co-operation of our non-resistance; hence it is best described as surrender. The great graces which God offers the soul in the first stages of spiritual growth tend to strengthen and dispose the will to make this surrender complete and perfect. Above all, the sacrament of Confirmation has this effect, but it is by no means inevitable that the Second Conversion must follow Confirmation. The sacramental grace and the Gifts of the Holy Ghost dispose the will to surrender but do not force it.

Before the Second Conversion the truths of religion and the reasons for being religious may be very much taken for granted, and there is no great sense of personal responsibility for the needs of the soul. It is rather as a child takes for granted the provision of the necessities for his bodily health and development but does not feel responsible for providing for himself, and is only too pleased to accept all that is provided for him without giving much thought to why it is done or whence it comes. In much the same way the soul in its first stages really does enjoy religion and is grateful for the provision God makes, but it has not as yet developed a sufficient sense of spiritual responsibility for God to reveal what is His due in return. All that God asks is the unconditional surrender of our will.

The Parallel Stages

Growing up is not merely a matter of physical development and change. There must be a proportionate development of mind and will. We expect a child to begin to acquire the elements of a sense of responsibility and at least to give some thought to the fact that the day is approaching when he will have to provide for himself. If a child does not develop in his mind and will proportionately to his physical age he is deemed an idiot or mentally defective. 'It is at this point that the analogy becomes illuminating for the spiritual life. We shall see that the beginner who fails to become a proficient, either turns to sin or else presents an example of arrested spiritual development. Here, too, it is true that "he who makes no progress loses ground", as the Fathers of the Church have so often pointed out' (Garrigou-Lagrange, op. cit., p.27).

The parallel stage in the spiritual life is our Second Conversion, and failure to make this normal development leaves the soul spiritually defective or *abnormal.* Hence there can be no grounds for spiritual pride in imagining ourselves privileged, above the normal, or any such foolishness, because we have passed through or are passing through this stage. Still less should we allow ourselves to become depressed or full of fears of vice and weakness because of the darkness and temptations which afflict the soul during it. All this is perfectly normal and must be experienced if our soul is to grow, as all life must grow, proportionately from stage to stage.

With converts this Second Conversion may coincide with their embracing the true Faith, but it is by no means always so. Their conversion to the Catholic Faith may arise from good motives but not the perfect one of unconditional surrender to the will of God. In this case, provided the convert has made the normal spiritual development, already described, to spiritual childhood, the Second Conversion will occur later and follow the same lines as for so-called bom Catholics. It is sometimes mistaken for the wearing off of first fervour, whereas, if it is rightly understood, it is really a sign of proper and normal spiritual growth. Just as for any other soul, it is a crisis and may become the occasion of a relapse and loss of faith.

An Example

The effect of the Second Conversion will become clearer if we take an example. We all know how our Lord insists that the first and greatest commandment is 'Thou shalt love the Lord thy God with thy whole heart, and with thy whole soul, and with all thy strength', and together with its corollary, 'Thou shalt love thy neighbour as thyself', it sums up the whole law of God. Before our Second Conversion we presume that in some sense or other we are obeying this great commandment, but we do not ask ourselves very explicitly how, or what it involves. In fact, some secret reservations hidden deep in our heart may be revealed if it is put in a way which makes more explicit all its implications; for example, 'Lord, grant that I may love Thee always and then do with me what Thou wilt'. Or, 'Lord, I desire only Thy will; teach me to hate my own will'. This may show that we still love our own will *for its own sake.*

This is not the same as the realization of our failure to accept perfectly the will of God on every occasion, for all of us must acknowledge this, but it is failure even to desire the acceptance of God's will whatever it may be. Nor does it necessarily mean that we refuse to accept God's will in any particular point, but only that we have not definitely embraced it by unconditional surrender. We have not developed that sense of spiritual responsibility which makes us realize God's supreme rights over us in every phase and aspect of our lives. To some extent we are still keeping our supernatural and natural lives in water-tight compartments as though there were no necessity for the former to absorb and spiritualize the latter.

A State of Indecision

It is quite possible that a soul may continue for a long time in this state of indecision without falling into mortal sin, and thus losing the new supernatural life, but such a state cannot continue indefinitely if there is to be normal growth of the spiritual life. This becomes clearer if we consider for a moment why God made us: to know, love, and serve Him. To know a person is by no means the same as knowing about a person. We may know quite a lot about Napoleon, but we cannot know him. We know a person by having some kind of communication with him, usually speech, while we can know about him simply from hearsay, study, reading, and gaining information one way or another about his life and character. We may know quite a lot about God from our religious instruction, but we can know God only through prayer. Hence the importance of a life of prayer and the necessity of taking this seriously as a prerequisite of the

Second Conversion. Before God can convert our will to Himself we must at least have begun to know Him. If prayer is neglected or is nothing more than mere formality bred of habit, we cannot learn to know God better and may even cease to know Him at all.

To love and serve God amounts to the same thing, for Christ says 'If you love Me, keep My commandments' (Jn 14:15). The object of the Second Conversion is to elicit from us an explicit act of love of God above all things, which will exclude any secret reservations which may perhaps have been hidden from ourselves. This is essentially an act of the will determining to obey God before all things by converting our own will into perfect harmony with God's. Before our Second Conversion we may be satisfied with making acts of love without much consideration of what they imply, and may be complacent about our spiritual state so long as we feel a certain amount of devotion in our prayers. It is this feeling of devotion which is so misleading and dangerous, as we may come to mistake it for true spirituality, relying on it almost entirely, and even making it the test of the objective truth of the Faith. Thus, when it loses its savour we may no longer feel any satisfaction in or desire for religion, and fear that we are receding and losing our faith.

Feelings of Emotion

As long as we are moved by this desire for satisfaction and feelings of devotion we are not offering to God a pure act of our will. Self is still intermingled in our choice and in choosing God we are still to some extent choosing self. If we remember that *what God wants is not our emotions but our will,* we will see why the first sign of the Second Conversion must be loss of feelings of devotion and pleasure in our religious life. God made me to love Him, and that means that God made me to give Him my will and not merely to *feel* devout and loving towards Him. Feelings of devotion, in the right sense of *affective* love, may come and grow intense in later stages of the spiritual life, and they may, in a somewhat less spiritual form, buoy us up during the first stages. They must, however, be sacrificed for a period lest they mislead us, while God is converting our soul to make a pure act of the will, that act of unconditional surrender to His supreme dominion over us, which is called *effective* love.

This period may be prolonged even for years and souls are frequently grieved and worried by their apparent loss of devotion. There is no need to worry so long as there is no deliberate consent to sin and the various duties and exercises of religion are fulfilled as well as possible in the circumstances. This coldness and feeling of aloofness from God is definitely a sign of growing up like the shyness and lack of responsiveness which so often afflicts children in their middle teens. They appear to lose their self-confidence, and that assurance of manner with others, which they had when younger, and might easily imagine that they were becoming less grown-up rather than developing into youth.

God wants the unconditional surrender of our will; not the passive surrender of the will-less but the active surrender of the willing. Hence we must do the choosing and must have a choice to make. God could overwhelm us with His own perfect lovableness and attractiveness so that we could not help but choose Him, but this would be the passive surrender of the will-less, for our own will would make no effective choice. For this reason the Second Conversion is marked by a very great lack of emotional attraction to God and to religion and a grave temptation away from God, so that the choice becomes clear-cut and definite, forcing the will to make a positive act of willing surrender to God.

From what has been said above we can easily deduce the usual signs and forms of the Second Conversion, though they vary very much in intensity, duration, and detail. The signs are a loss of devotion and feeling in prayer; little comfort or satisfaction in religion or in the duties and exercises of the spiritual life; a feeling of praying into a void with no one to listen or care about our prayers; spiritual darkness and that weariness of religion that Fr Faber well describes as the monotony of piety. The truths of faith lose their reality and become formalities which give us little or no emotional response. This may be especially true of the Holy Eucharist, making our Holy Communions lack savour and feelings of devotion. Often there is a great loneliness, very like that which afflicts adolescents, and unwillingness to ask advice or discuss our difficulties with others. We feel that we must stand alone and fight our own battle without others, perhaps because we are still too egoistical and self-centred to imagine that anyone else could have suffered anything quite like what we are going through.

An Essential Characteristic

The form of this trial may vary but it must have one essential characteristic, it must offer the will a definite choice. In some way or other we are faced with a choice between our own will and God's will, for the final outcome of the Second Conversion must be Christ's own prayer, 'Not my will, but Thine be done'. Hence common forms are: persistent and grave temptation to sin, or to reject what we know or seriously suspect to be the will of God for us. There may be temptations against faith, temptations against purity, temptations to refuse a vocation to the priesthood or religious life, or temptations to rebel against the will of God as manifested by some grave trouble or infirmity. These will not be merely passing or periodic temptations, such as all souls experience both before and after the Second Conversions, but persistent, gnawing, and intense. God does not send them, for 'God is not a tempter of evils; and He tempteth no man' (Jas 1:13), but He permits them as the occasion of our conversion, and no doubt the devil adds fuel to them. God permits them, as has already been said, to force us to make that explicit act of the will which really does amount to loving God with our whole heart and soul and above all things. Sanctifying Grace fills the soul with the infused gift of Charity which enables us to love God above all things, but this is not as yet explicit in all its implications. By the Second Conversion we face the question fairly and squarely and declare ourselves unreservedly for God.

A very common form of this crisis is temptation against

faith, and a more detailed examination of this one form will throw light on all. This is a particularly difficult one to bear because of the spiritual darkness, lack of feelings of devotion, and aridity, which always accompany the Second Conversion. Moreover, in what I have called our spiritual infancy and childhood we may have accepted and taken for granted the doctrines of our religion largely from emotional reasons. Consequently, not only must our will be converted, but our intellect must also be satisfied. The grace of faith must, of course, help in this, as it has always helped us to believe without doubting whatever God has revealed. But God does not ask or force anyone to act against human reason, but rather to rise above it and acknowledge that divine Truth must of its very infinity be more than finite mind can comprehend. Before we reach the crisis of our Second Conversion we may have believed to a large extent because it never entered our mind not to believe. Then, if we come up against arguments about religion and are forced into circumstances that demand conviction or complete loss of faith, God may well use these circumstances as the occasion for our Second Conversion by allowing grave temptations against faith to assail us.

A Pagan Environment

This is particularly frequent in these days when young people are being suddenly transferred from the Catholic atmosphere of good homes and schools into an almost pagan environment. Such an experience is almost bound to precipitate the crisis of the Second Conversion, and failure to pass through it successfully may well be the cause of some of those defections from the Faith among well-instructed and formerly devout Catholics to which I have referred. This falling away, however, is not fatal and complete through delay in making our surrender, as the state of indecision may last for years. There may even be some giving ground, some falling back and lapse into sin together with neglect of religious duties, while the fight is on. Nor, of course, even in a case of complete failure must we say there is no hope of salvation. God's mercy is boundless and we may be sure He yearns for our salvation even more vehemently than we can possibly desire it ourselves. 'God is faithful, who will not suffer you to be tempted above that which you are able; but will make also with temptation issue, that you may be able to bear it' (1 Cor. 10:13).

How are we to meet this crisis of our spiritual life? The first and all-important point is to realize that it is a state or stage in the *normal* growth of the new supernatural life of the soul. To know this is more than half the battle, and for this reason it has seemed to me worth while attempting to give this little account of it. For once we are aware why God permits these trials we can see what we must aim at doing. God wants *our will,* which is the same as our love. Hence the counter-action required on our part must be in our will. We should not waste time trying to stir up feelings of devotion by feverishly trying out new forms of piety, but fix our will on doing as well as possible, however coldly and unsatisfyingly, what we have been accustomed to do in the way of spiritual exercises. The time for increasing the amount and advancing to higher forms of prayer comes later; for the present it is enough that we give the time we have usually given to praying as best we can, though this in our arid state may seem a very poor best. We must, of course, pray earnestly for grace to meet the crisis and our prayer should tend to become more and more simple acts of the will rather than the emotional rhetoric of some books of devotion. We cannot do better than follow our Lord's example by repeating over and over again the self-same prayer that happens to suit our mood. 'Lord, teach me to love Thy will.' 'Lord, enlighten my mind.' 'Lord, help my unbelief.' 'Lord, not my will, but Thine be done.'

God to Decide

Secondly, we must not allow ourselves to be overwhelmed with the fruitless effort of trying to satisfy our mind on every little point. For example, one could argue incessantly for and against the reality of one's vocation to the priesthood or religious life without coming to any decision. We must decide in our will that, whatever the arguments against a vocation may be, if God wills me to be a priest or religious I am His to command. If once we start questioning 'Am I fit or worthy?' the answer must be 'Of course not'. But then, who is? We must leave it to God to decide.

When the temptations are against faith the principle still remains the same, that we must concentrate on the will rather than on satisfying the intellect or emotions. Faith is not a matter of feeling or emotional acceptance of religious doctrines based on some vague assumptions, such as many non-Catholics seem to think, and so it is an absolute waste of time to try to make our imagination feel the truth of such mysteries as the Real Presence. It is objectively true for rational reasons, but, as it is above reason, we need an act of the will to accept it and, of course, above all, the grace of God. If we can rise to the supreme act of the will, sweeping aside all the difficulties and doubts that beset the mind during our temptations against faith, and say 'I believe', we have made our surrender to God and won the day.

This, however, may not always be possible when a soul may have given too much ground to be able to make such an act of faith. It may be necessary to satisfy the intellect by establishing anew the rational principles for the acceptance of the Catholic Church as our infallible teacher before the will can make its act of faith. In this case we must stress the point that it is the fundamental principles that must be studied and not waste our time seeking to solve every point and detail, or to answer every argument advanced by unbelievers. The principles which I would suggest for consideration are: God; Christ is God, therefore Christ's religion and Church are divine; but what is divine must be true; to be true Christ's Church must be infallible; only the Catholic Church claims to be infallible and has the other marks we must expect in a religion founded by God. There are numerous books dealing with these points, but any well-instructed Catholic should know the arguments and it should only be a question of recalling them and satisfying the intellect as to their validity. Good will and the grace of God will do the rest. All other doctrines of faith can then be accepted on the infallible authority of the Church without seeking to settle every difficulty and objection to them individually.

This does not mean that detailed study of our religion is not important but only that times of temptation against faith are not the moment for it. Later, we will benefit far more from deeper studies, which will lead to a real appreciation of the Faith. If every difficulty were solved, every *t* crossed and *i* dotted to the satisfaction of the intellect, there would be no need for an act of the will in accepting the Faith, and so the conversion, which is essentially an act of the will, could not result from these temptations against faith. Without this conversion of our will we cannot grow up normally in our spiritual life but will remain spiritually deficient. 'Just as the child who does not grow does not merely remain a child but becomes an idiot, so the beginner who does not enter upon the way of proficients when he ought to, does not merely remain a beginner, but becomes a stunted soul. It would seem, unhappily, that the great majority of souls do not belong to any of these three categories, of beginners, proficients, or perfect, but rather of stunted souls!' (Garrigou-Lagrange, op. cit., p.38). We must make up our minds to make our unconditional surrender and not remain in a state of wavering indecision. Failure to do so may spell spiritual disaster and total ruin for the soul, or, at best, a poor mediocrity and tepidity in the practice of religion, which will become a burden and a bore. The joy of religion comes only to generous souls, and this is the first really great act of generosity that God asks of us.

Complete Surrender

God cannot ask for less than complete surrender, for He is all in all and must have supreme dominion over us, either by the loving acceptance of His rule, or by our rebellious submission to His just judgment. To ask God to share His throne with our miserable self-love is blasphemy. God does not put every soul to this crucial test; some He allows gradually to grow in generosity until they are actually giving themselves wholly to Him without realizing that they have made their unconditional surrender to His holy will. Just as He calls certain souls, for His own good reasons, to the priesthood or religious life, while leaving others apparently much better fitted for such a vocation, so He selects some souls for the crucial test and leaves others, equally spiritual, to develop gradually and imperceptibly. We may be sure, however, that He is offering to the chosen soul a very great grace in return for their formal act of surrender, and to refuse a great grace is often to lose all grace. On the other hand God never asks us to do anything beyond our powers and will always give abundant grace to enable us to fulfil His holy will.

We must beware of expecting exaggerated effects from the spiritual experience that I have attempted to describe, for the Second Conversion is really only the first step in a serious interior life, the passing from childhood to adolescence.

It must destroy all affection for mortal sin and form in us a habit or facility in making the necessary sacrifices for avoiding mortal sin. This in itself is a tremendous step forward and must result in an ever-increasing generosity in the service of God. Interiorly there is a great transformation in our attitude towards God and religion, but this may not be very perceptible outwardly or even to ourselves. We may not realize that we have passed through this crisis until long afterwards, when we can look back and recognize this transformation in the importance which we attach to spiritual duties and practices, with a correspondingly greater faithfulness to them.

An Awareness of God

After our Second Conversion our religion ceases to be merely one aspect or part of our lives among several, and becomes our whole life, so that all our judgments and valuation are spiritualized by it. We develop an awareness of God which cannot easily be described. It is not vision, nor feeling, nor inspiration, but a deep, inescapable certainty of mind and will that God is with us even when the soul is steeped in spiritual darkness, aridity, and dullness. There is still a long road ahead with many trials and possibly falls, but God has revealed Himself to us by His Spirit. 'Now, we have received not the spirit of this world, but the Spirit that is of God; that we may know the things that are given us from God. Which things also we speak; not in the learned words of human wisdom, but in the doctrine of the Spirit, comparing spiritual things with spiritual. But the sensual man perceiveth not these things that are of the Spirit of God. For it is foolishness to him; and he cannot understand, because it is spiritually examined. But the spiritual man judgeth all things; and he himself is judged of no man. For who hath known the mind of the Lord, that He may instruct him? But we have the mind of Christ' (1 Cor. 2:12–16).

BACKGROUND

Caryll Houselander's *Christ within Me* is a compressed meditation on the humility of God, who comes to us in the form of bread and uses what seem to us trivial and insignificant things, the routine monotonies and despairs of daily life, so as to be present, through us, to the world. Her writing is wholly original; Ronald Knox, after reading her, wrote her the only fan-letter of his life.

Delia Smith writes on an apparently less exalted level; but her message, of simplicity and making time for God to act in us, rather than feeling we have to do something, is a profound one.

Herbert Fincham's *Second Conversion* is on one level a technical treatise about the mystical life; but on another, it reminds us that our initial turning to God, whatever form it took, needs to be renewed by a deeper and more honest welcoming of God's life into every part of ours.

CTS ONEFIFTIES

1. FR DAMIEN & WHERE ALL ROADS LEAD · *Robert Louis Stevenson & G K Chesterton*

2. THE UNENDING CONFLICT · *Hilaire Belloc*

3. CHRIST UPON THE WATERS · *John Henry Newman*

4. DEATH & RESURRECTION · *Leonard Cheshire VC & Bede Jarrett OP*

5. THE DAY THE BOMB FELL · *Johannes Siemes SJ & Bruce Kent*

6. MIRACLES · *Ronald Knox*

7. A CITY SET ON A HILL · *Robert Hugh Benson*

8. FINDING THE WAY BACK · *Francis Ripley*

9. THE GUNPOWDER PLOT · *Herbert Thurston SJ*

10. NUNS – WHAT ARE THEY FOR? · *Maria Boulding OSB, Bruno Webb OSB & Jean Cardinal Daniélou SJ*

11. ISLAM, BRITAIN & THE GOSPEL · *John Coonan, William Burridge & John Wijngaards*

12. STORIES OF THE GREAT WAR · *Eileen Boland*

13. LIFE WITHIN US · *Caryll Houselander, Delia Smith & Herbert Fincham*

14. INSIDE COMMUNISM · *Douglas Hyde*

15. COURTSHIP: SOME PRACTICAL ADVICE · *Anon, Hubert McEvoy SJ, Tony Kirwin & Malcolm Brennan*

16. RESURRECTION · *Vincent McNabb OP & B C Butler OSB*

17. TWO CONVERSION STORIES · *James Britten & Ronald Knox*

18. MEDIEVAL CHRISTIANITY · *Christopher Dawson*

19. A LIBRARY OF TALES – VOL 1 · *Lady Herbert of Lea*

20. A LIBRARY OF TALES – VOL 2 · *Eveline Cole & E Kielty*

21. WAR AT HOME AND AT THE FRONT · *"A Chaplain" & Mrs Blundell of Crosby*

22. THE CHURCH & THE MODERN AGE · *Christopher Hollis*

23. THE PRAYER OF ST THÉRÈSE OF LISIEUX · *Vernon Johnson*

24. THE PROBLEM OF EVIL · *Martin D'Arcy SJ*

25. WHO IS ST JOSEPH? · *Herbert Cardinal Vaughan*